Authorship is no longer the vocation of the elite.
Authorship is a necessity for every career.
Authorship is a natural passion.

PUBLISH

IT

NOW

I0203276

The internet and new publishing technologies have
made it possible for inspired newcomers to compete on
the same playing field with seasoned professionals

Rodney Charles

Publish It Now

Rodney Charles

© Rodney Charles 2006

Published by 1stWorld Publishing
1100 North 4th St. Suite 131, Fairfield, Iowa 52556
tel: 641-209-5000 • fax: 641-209-3001
web: www.1stworldpublishing.com

First Edition

LCCN: 2006903923
SoftCover ISBN: 1595408452
HardCover ISBN: 1595408444
eBook ISBN: 1595408460
Color SoftCover ISBN: 1595408479
Color HardCover ISBN: 1595408487

With Appreciation for:

Tim Mahaney Ed Spinella
Shawna Baird Anuj Mathur
Diane Frank Tony Ellis
Liz Howard Brianna Delott
Brad Fregger Barbara Foley Christine Schrum
Ravi Badhwar Anya Charles Aman Charles
Most of all Nandini Charles, my bride and co-adventurer

Special thanks to Dan Poynter and John Kremer for helping me every step of the way. What I have learned and taught about writing, publishing, distribution and marketing has been influenced by two undisputed mentors in the Publishing Industry: Dan Poynter and John Kremer, from whom I have borrowed heavily throughout this book. For anyone planning a career in writing or publishing, it is essential to digest the volumes of material these two pioneers have collected and organized

www.parapublishing.com Dan Poynter
www.bookmarket.com John Kremer

This simple book was written to:

INSPIRE

EDUCATE

ASSIST

Anyone who has ever dreamed of becoming a published author.

CONTENTS

Part 1: Inspiration

Part 2: A Good Book

Part 3: A Marketing Plan

Part 4: A Little Knowledge About the Publishing Industry

(A Tutorial for 1st World Publishing)

"With so many blockbuster self-published successes in the past few years, it is now safe to self-publish with respect. Publishers Weekly routinely reviews self-published books, something they would never have done five or ten years ago. Gone are the days ..."

—writes *Publishers Weekly* Rights Columnist **Paul Nathan**

"Many larger publishers now scour the Internet for self-published and POD books that could fit their publishing program."

—**John Kremer**, *Author of 1001 Ways to Market Your Book*

3 Essentials

There are 3 things that you need to succeed as a published author. And by succeed I mean earn enough money through book sales to allow you to continue writing full time.

1. INSPIRATION: You need to be inspired. Enthusiasm is capable of overcoming any obstacle.

2. A GOOD BOOK: Rewrite your book many times so the reader can feel the balanced rhythm, confidence and authority of your writing voice.

3. A MARKETING PLAN: How will readers know your book is available? You must tell them, tell them again and keep telling them every day.

If you are oozing with INSPIRATION you may still succeed.

If you have A GOOD BOOK and A MARKETING PLAN you just might succeed.

If you possess INSPIRATION, A GOOD BOOK and A MARKETING PLAN, you are sure to succeed.

PART 1
INSPIRATION

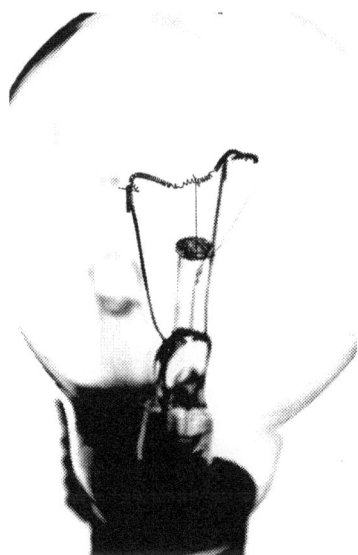

1

My Publishing Daze

I first decided to launch a career as an author in 1991. I lived in Fairfield, Iowa, and I didn't have a dime. I had passed the previous 14 years of my life as a monk in upstate New York, and having graduated from the life of spiritual development, I couldn't possibly have been more naive about the ways of the world.

It didn't take long to figure out that I had better find a way to make some money or I'd soon be fighting over sidewalk space with my local streetpeople.

I found a way to eke out a living buying and selling artwork, while at night during my travels, I was writing a manuscript—which, like all authors, I knew was the greatest literary work ever created.

Having spent so many years as a monk, I naturally had a passion for the lives of saints. I read hundreds of biographies (possibly thousands) and compiled brief accounts of their lives into a story-a-day book called EVERY DAY A MIRACLE HAPPENS.

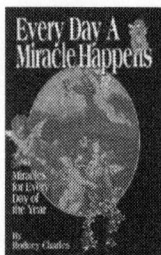

I just knew that publishers were going to be franticly fighting over the right to publish this masterpiece. I could see each publisher bidding higher and higher in the millions, offering record-breaking advanced royalties.

Alas, it did not happen.

Not only did I receive dozens of "form-generated-rejection letters," but even family and friends felt in necessary to elucidate my delusions.

Of course, this was madness! I could hardly believe there were so many publishers incapable of recognizing my idiomatic literary genius. Who knew!

So I devised a plan. I would publish EVERY DAY A MIRACLE HAPPENS myself. After all, how hard could it be and how could I deprive the world of this modern masterpiece?

There was, however, one small problem: I didn't have any money. In fact, I had no credit history. I had never owned a credit card, taken out a loan, owned a mortgage and until a year or so before, I had never had a bank account (one of the benefits of monkhood).

The next day, I visited the bank to ask for my first loan, waving my 600-page manuscript in hand. The loan officers were aghast that my name didn't even appear in any of the credit systems so they respectfully laughed me right out of the bank.

Rejected, I got in my car and started to drive until an idea hit me. I WILL PRE-SELL MY MASTERPIECE!!!

About forty minutes of research in the local public library gave me the names and addresses of all the bookstores and distributors within a 4 hour drive of Fairfield, Iowa.

I formatted my book using an elementary word processing program so it looked like a real "trade-sized" book and printed out a color copy of a self-designed cover which I pasted over the formatted pages. Squinting at it from a very long distance, it looked almost like a real book.

Touting my mockup book, I drove to every distributor in my area and visited with all the regional buyers for the Barnes and Noble chain of stores. My enthusiasm was infectious and I promised to do book signings in all of their stores once the book was in print (a promise that I kept).

Before 2 weeks had passed, I solicited over 2,400 orders for my book and I had the purchase orders and book order requests on bookstore stationary to support it.

I returned to the same loan officer and said "Let's do the math"

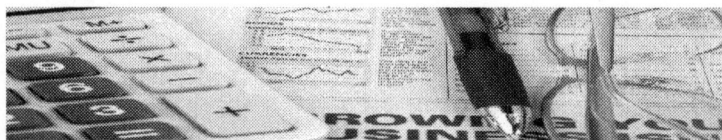

He looked over the purchase orders, slapped himself on his forehead and said, "I am going to regret this" (but he never did). He issued me a loan for $12.000,which was enough money to print 3,000 copies of my book. My publishing career had begun.

There is no describing the feeling of holding your first published book in your hand. In my mind, I saw hoards of people pushing and shoving at the entrances to bookstores, eager to snatch up the last remaining copy of my masterpiece.

But it never happened. In fact nothing happened, until I realized that EVEN THOUGH MY BOOK WAS AVAIL-ABLE EVERYWHERE, NO ONE KNEW ABOUT IT.

I had very little money at that time, but I just knew my book was the cure for the plague that ravaged the ailing masses, so off I set to let them know that the end to their literary starvation was only a book away.

I mentioned earlier that no one could have been more ignorant of the publishing industry than I, so my plan was very simple: drive to every city where I had family or friends who wouldn't mind my visit, and set up book signings and free talks at the local libraries. For the most part, my plan worked quite well, but it was far more work than I had imagined. After I set up an event in a city, I opened the local YellowPages and called every TV, radio and print media listing I could find. The first few cities were the most difficult. Most media people declined my promotions, but I was still able to set up three or four announcements, author interviews, book reviews or articles, and that started the ball rolling. Once I had some press clippings in my resumé I created a media kit and each successive city got easier and easier to promote. People were finding out about my book and it was starting to sell, independent of my efforts.

> "Every Day A Miracle Happens is an easy read and a good choice in its field, that's also light and fun."
>
> **—Publishers Weekly**

My break came when I finally drafted a letter to *Publishers Weekly*, ignorantly pleading that I simply did not understand the conventions of the publishing industry and would they please consider my book for review even though I did not submit a galley copy to them four months prior to the publication date. My book ended up on the desk of Phyllis Tickle, the religion editor for *Publishers Weekly*, who took a risk, broke convention and gave EVERY DAY A MIRACLE HAPPENS a superb review. This single review catalyzed numerous unsolicited reviews from other reviewers and was ultimately responsible for placing my book on regional and national bestsellers lists.

What I didn't know was that success has its own set of problems. My book was in demand, so I needed to print more and more copies. I was taking orders, managing print runs, shipping and fulfilling orders, warehousing, billing, doing customer service, managing collections of accounts receivable, processing returns, etc, etc. There was absolutely no time for marketing and promotions and no time to complete the second book of my dreams.

****

The abridged version of this story is ... 1st World Publishing was the response to this dilemma. Combining the author services required for success, I created a publishing company for every author. 1st World Publishing is a complete publishing house that takes care of the many details of the publishing industry and allows authors to be writers who maintain control over the outcome of their books.

Given my background in this industry, I naturally have a personal prejudice toward self publishing. Authors should make as much or more profit from their books as publishers do. Why not? They do all the work. But the long and short of it is: you can get what you want out of 1st World Publishing. Your level of success is directly proportional to your determination.

3.

notice.

pub/lic

d to se-

offices, paid for by

of being

[1670–80]

owledge.

Pub/lic Works/ Ad

PUBLIC,

agency (1933–44) that

jects for the construc

P.W.A.

to give

hey publi-

pub•lish (pub/lish),

esp. Brit.,

wise reproduced tex

software, etc.) for sa

issue publicly the

Faulkner. **3.** to

ublic stat-

claim; promulgate

that applies

known. **5.** Law.

branch of

ent) to some pe

2

Self-Publishing:
An Honorable Undertaking

Stephanie Dircks Ashcraft never expected to sell thousands of copies of *101 Things to Do with a Cake Mix*. In mid-October 2002, the 2nd edition had hit #9 on the *New York Times* paperback advice bestseller list.

In 1998, **Arthur Agatston,** author of *The South Beach Diet,* began by self-publishing several hundred pamphlets outlining his diet ideas for patients. Several years later, he has sold almost seven million copies.

Amanda Brown's self-published first novel, *Legally Blonde,* was made into the 2001 hit movie starring Reese Witherspoon.

Ken Blanchard and **Spencer Johnson** originally self-published *The One-Minute Manager* so they could sell the book for $15 at a time when all the experts were telling them they'd never sell the book for such a high price. In three months' time, they sold over 20,000 copies in the San Diego area alone. *The One-Minute Manager* has sold more than 12 million copies and been published in 25+ languages.

Tami Oldham Ashcraft self-published her story of surviving Hurricane Raymond out in the Pacific Ocean (*Red Sky in Mourning*). After selling more than 8,000 copies of her edition, she sold the reprint rights for half a million dollars.

Craig Alesse began *Amherst Media* by self-publishing his own how-to photography books. His company is now one of the premiere how-to photography publishing companies in the world, distributing to photography stores across the country.

Mary Appelhof self-published *Worms Eat My Garbage.* Her first edition sold more than 100,000 copies. In 1997, she published her second edition.

Bestselling Canadian author **Margaret Atwood** self-published her first volume of poetry *Double Persephone* the year she graduated from college. The print run was only 200 copies. Atwood has gone on to become a bestselling novelist and short story writer.

In the fall of 2004, **Joe Babcock,** winner of the Writer's Digest International Self-Published book award, sold rights to his novel *The Tragedy of Miss Geneva Flowers* to Carroll & Graf.

Cheryl and Peter Barnes started up Vacation Spot Books by self-publishing Peter's children's book, *Nat, Nat, the Nantucket Cat,* in 1992. In 2001, Cheryl met Mattie J.T. Stepanek, a child poet suffering from a rare form of muscular dystrophy, while working as a volunteer at Washington, D.C.'s Children's Hospital. Inspired by his spirit and poems, she went on to publish several collections of his poems. *Heartsongs* and *Journey Through Heartsongs* both made it to the *New York Times* bestseller list.

John Bartlett financed and self-published the first three editions of *Familiar Quotations,* the bestselling quote book on the market.

L. Frank Baum self-published at least some of the books in the *Wizard of Oz* series.

❖

In 2000, after getting 70 rejections for his comic novel, screenwriter **John Blumenthal** self-published a trade paperback of *What's Wrong with Dorfman?*, which was selected by *January Magazine* as one of the 50 best books of 2000. He went on to get more major reviews and finally sold the book for a substantial sum of money.

❖

Richard N. Bolles originally self-published *What Color Is Your Parachute?* as a small typed guide for Episcopal priests who needed to readjust after leaving the priesthood. The book has now spent 288 weeks on the *New York Times* bestseller list and returns to other bestseller lists (such as *Business Week's*) each year when a new edition comes out.

❖

Australian dietician **Allan Borushek** has sold more than 11 million copies of his self-published calorie counter books and other products in the U.S. and Australia. About 8 million copies were sold in Australia, which is a remarkable feat considering Australia has a population equivalent to Texas.

❖

H. Jackson Brown originally self-published his renowned *Life's Little Instruction Book.* He went on to sell more than 5 million copies and made the bestseller lists for both hardcover and soft-cover books.

Paula Begoun self-published her first book, *Blue Eye Shadow Should Be Illegal,* a how-to book on using the right cosmetics. She followed the success of her first book with *Don't Go to the Cosmetics Counter Without Me* and *Don't Go Shopping for Hair Care Products Without Me.* These three beauty books have sold more than two million copies.

Nick Bunick self-published *The Messengers* by Julia Ingram and G.W. Hardin in 1996. This nonfiction book tells the true story of Bunick and his experiences with angels and reincarnation. He spent $160,000 promoting it, which led to selling the rights to *Pocket Books* for $1,000,000.00 a few months later.

William Byham self-published the bestselling business book, *Zapp: The Lightning of Empowerment,* which has sold more than 2.5 million copies to date.

Before selling rights to Putnam, **Julia Cameron** self-published her bestselling *The Artist's Way.* The book has sold more than a million copies to date.

Professional gambler **Avery Cardoza** built a publishing empire writing and publishing gambling advice books. In 2003, he self-published a new magazine, *Avery Cardoza's Player*, for the amateur gambler.

Richard Carlson, author of the bestselling *Don't Sweat the Small Stuff series,* began his book career by self-publishing *The Business of Bodywork.*

Cindy Cashman and **Alan Garner,** self-published *Everything Men Know about Women* (using the pseudonym of Dr. Alan Francis) and sold more than half a million copies of the blank book before selling rights to Andrews McMeel. The book has now sold more than 1.5 million copies.

Novelist **Willa Cather** paid for the publication of her first novel, *One of Ours,* which went on to win the Pulitzer Prize.

Dave Chilton self-published *The Wealthy Barber* and dedicated himself to doing hundreds of interviews during that first year. His book had made the Canadian bestseller list in 1991 and remained there until 1996. His book is the bestselling book in Canadian history, excluding the Bible.

Deepak Chopra vanity published his first book and then sold the rights to Crown Publishing. The book went on to become the first of many *New York Times* bestsellers for him.

Wade Cook self-published many of his bestselling books, including Stock Market Miracles and Wall Street Money Machine.

Laura Corn self-published *101 Nights of Grrreat Sex* and several other books. She sold 100,000 copies of *237 Intimate Questions Every Woman Should Ask a Man* from the trunk of her car. Total sales for *101 Nights* was 525,000 copies as of March 1999.

PART 2
A GOOD BOOK

3

Whatever You Love the Most…
Write About It!

I do not regard myself to be an extraordinary writer. But through writing, marketing books, and teaching writing workshops for the past ten years, I have come to

> "If a man can write a better book, preach a better sermon, or make a better mousetrap than his neighbor, though he builds his house in the woods, the world will make a beaten path to his door."
>
> **—Ralph Waldo Emerson**

conclude what many before me have: the single key to success is to "write what you know."

Unfortunately the "write what you know" axiom tends to confuse many new writers, so I would like to offer this explanation to clarify:

First and foremost the writing process is a way of getting in touch with what you really know. So ask yourself: what do I really know? What fascinates me, inspires me, makes me want to share my story with others?

Good writing is all about honesty. Successful writers know they are the only experts on their own lives, and when they draw from a reservoir of simple honesty, their thoughts, feelings, and imaginings somehow become infused with universal relevance. And that's something readers pick up on immediately.

My intention here is not to educate you on how to be a writer (I'll leave that journey to you), but rather to inspire you to:

1. Get started writing or keep your momentum going
2. Understand the importance of proper editing
3. Get your writing published and sold

There are thousands of good books available that can help you to develop and hone your writing skills. I suggest that you find the ones that resonate deeply with you and inspire you to read them over and over again.

If you are not the type to learn from books, there are plenty of writers' workshops available in nearly every city or town in the USA and abroad.

As a general rule, if you intend to be good at what you do, you must practice your craft a little bit every day. Repetition is the singular key to perfection in any field.

Everyone's process is different. I have seen brilliant writers who can perform brain surgery for 8 hours a day and return home to write a book at the dining table with 7 wildly normal children interrupting every sentence. I have known other brilliant writers who can only write in total reclusion, miles from the nearest homestead. The point is, it doesn't matter what your personality dictates. Just start the writing process and stay with it. Writing, and especially rewriting, has a way of clearing away your pretensions and leaving only the good stuff behind.

> "I was working on the proof of one of my poems all the morning, and took out a comma. In the afternoon I put it back again."
>
> **—Oscar Wilde**

So try to write about "what you know" every day. My standard line for teaching creative writing workshops is: "Write as fast as you can and never look back." Correct nothing as you create a first draft. Just write and enjoy. Riding the wave of inspiration at the beginning of a written work and not getting caught up in the mechanics of writing is one of the biggest hurdles to overcome. Many aspiring writers never make it to the second stage of writing, which is editing, because they diffuse their initial inspiration by fussing over details and grammar too early in the writing project. Many never even finish their first drafts. Don't let this happen to you! Hang in there. It's worth it in the long run.

Once you have exhausted your supply of experiences, insights and imaginings and your first draft is complete, the refining process can begin. That's where the magic happens. This is when other people (writers and editors) enter into the process, and not a moment before. (Note: Generally it is a good idea to refine your work *before* you show it to non-writers. If someone does not understand the wonderfully chaotic nature of first drafts, they may inadvertently dilute your enthusiasm.) Writing, for the most part is a community project, not a solitary profession, and it is a good idea to clean up your work before showing it around. You will find yourself learning and borrowing from many authors …and this is as it should be.

> The faster I write the better my output. If I'm going slow, I'm in trouble. It means I'm pushing the words instead of being pulled by them.
>
> **—Raymond Chandler**

But remember, the first step is to "write what you know." Whatever YOU LOVE THE MOST, write about that. When you do, you will find it is hard to stop writing and readers will find it hard to stop reading your work. This is the FIRST step to creating a good book. All the remaining steps are the process of fine-tuning and refinement. And that's where EDITING comes in…

> "If the doctor told me I had six minutes to live, I'd type a little faster."
>
> **—Isaac Asimov**

COFFEE

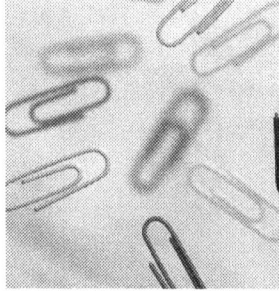

4

Editing

CLARITY and ORGANIZATION are paramount in a finished work. Typos and grammatical errors will detract from your message and ruin your credibility as an author. Mistakes may also cost you significant time and money when you have to repair them after your book is in print. A poorly edited book can spoil a great project, so don't let typographical errors, bad grammar or structural problems besmirch your work. Even the most meticulously researched and thoughtfully written works will fail to impress readers if they are riddled with typos and structural flaws.

Many authors bring their books to me saying, "My book is thoroughly edited." As a rule, I usually ask if the work has been edited by a family member or friend. If the answer is yes, I normally recommend another edit by someone outside the author's immediate circle of influence. EVERY AUTHOR NEEDS an objective eye to pick out irrelevant repetitions, grammatical errors and spelling mistakes that the untrained eye often overlooks. A good editor will supply you with a carefully checked, completely corrected end product, free of inconsistencies.

> Many modern novels have a beginning, a muddle and an end.
>
> **—Philip Larkin**

If you are writing nonfiction, INDEXING is important. Indexing is the art of organizing information. Indexes point readers or users to the information they are seeking. A good index allows readers to quickly find what they are looking for without poring over each page. The indexer is responsible for reading through the manuscript and not only selecting key terms within the book, but also selecting key concepts. Once the indexer has a clear grasp of the book's terms and concepts, he or she will then create and organize an index suitable to the book's audience.

If you need an editor or indexer, you can find a host of trained professionals at www.1stworldpublish.com.

1st World's team of skilled experts can meticulously proof essays, term papers, dissertations, thesis, textbooks, general books, journal papers, reports, manuals, scientific papers, medical documents, technology papers, and more. Let us assist you in polishing your work.

> "It is perfectly okay to write garbage—as long as you edit brilliantly."
>
> **—Oscar Wilde**

5

The New Art of Writing and Publishing Your Book

The process of book writing and publishing has changed forever. Today's authors are researching, writing, producing, selling and promoting their books themselves. Everyone is jumping on board-from major publishers like Barnes & Noble and Random House, to well-known authors and first-time writers. Now virtually anyone can break into the publishing industry faster, easier and cheaper. Rapid advancements in technology and distribution techniques have opened the doors to a new era of publishing-one that favors authors.

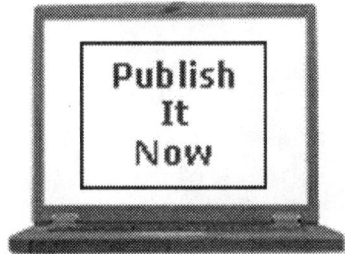

Gone are the days of stacks of manuscript pages with double-spaced lines. Today's manuscripts look like books. Computers, the internet and new software programs have changed the way we write books and the way we publish them.

Today, authors "build" their books; writing is just part of the assembly. Modern authors have more options, visual aids and research tools to help them share their unique message with their readers. With today's technologies, authors like you can add literary quotes, digital photos and scanned drawings to you're their manuscript as they write, (see www.1stworldpublishing.com) You pull information from the Web, add resource URLs to your text, search encyclopedias for background information, go to art sites for illustrations and quotation sites for quotations, and much more. All these visual-aid resources are available to you as you draft your manuscript. See www.1stworld-publishing.com/art-resources

Once the content of your book is set up (hopefully you will have improved and rewritten the work many times since you first set out), it is time for an editor to help out. You will save time if you submit your completed manuscript to your copy editor via email, or rewritable CD (to find an editor, see www.1stworldpublishing.com/editor). Have the editor make changes on the file and return it to you. Then re-read the manuscript to make sure the editor has improved the copy without making content changes that don't suit you. If the corrections are made to a printout (the old way), you will have to enter the changes and then proof the changes. This is time consuming and there are more opportunities for error, but it may be your only option. (If you know you have something to say and you feel you just can't get it down on paper, consider hiring a writer: www.1stworldpublishing.com/professional-writers.) Professional writers are hired every day by business professionals, celebrities, politicians or school teachers who require an authored book (or articles) to assist them in advancing their careers.)

Following this new model for writing, your manuscript will grow, looking like a proper book from the start. Then, as easy as sending an email you can submit your manuscript to 1st World Publishing and we will walk you through every step of the publishing process (see www.1stworldpublishing.com).

Now, if you like, you can maximize the value of your work by repurposing your content into other products. Those versions may be for Web-based downloadable books, ebooks, compact discs, articles, special reports, your personal blog site, seminars, consulting and digital audio. See the Publishers and Author's Directory at www.1stworldpublishing.com/directory.

Electronic editions of your book may have even more features than the print version: they may have color illustrations, sound, video and hyperlinks. Your e-edition will take up less space, be even less expensive to produce and will provide a richer experience to your reader (see www.1stworldpublshing.com/publishitnowebook).

Producing Your Book

Publishing a book in print is now just an option, and a good one if you have a large prepublication demand, such as advanced sales to bookstores and/or a sale to a bookclub. But if you don't already have a long list of buyers, there is no reason to print thousands of copies of your book on spec, hoping to sell the inventory. In the future, most books will not be manufactured until after they are sold.

There is a Better Way: POD

Print-On-Demand (one book at a time) is the way of the future. Very soon it may be the only print technology employed. Here is why:

1. Tens, perhaps hundreds of millions of books (the equivalent of an entire forest) are destroyed every year due to over-runs and remainders. Warehouses are bursting with books that did not sell and which are too costly to ship, even for charitable purposes. In the end, they are destroyed. With POD there is no wastage, no warehousing, no loss of investment and no insurance hassles. Whatever is ordered by the consumer is produced by the manufacturer.

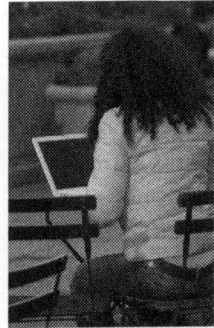

2. With POD printing, authors may send their finished books to agents and publishers. A finished book leaves a far

better impression and if a sales record has been established, your agent's job is significantly easier. With POD, authors and publishers can test the waters carefully. They may send copies to reviewers, distributors, catalogs, specialty stores, associations, book clubs, premium prospects, foreign publishers and others. When I self-published my first book (in the olden days), I had to pre-sell 2,400 copies before I could afford to send my book to press. But with POD making the printing process so simple and affordable, books no longer need to be produced in great quantities in the hopes they'll be sold at a future date. Soon all books will be produced at the exact time they are needed. POD production offers lower investment costs, no inventory concerns, plus custom publishing and quicker reprints. Today, Print-On-Demand is forging its way to dominance.

3. With POD, now almost everyone can afford to publish. In the recent past the cost of commercial printing was simply too high. Compare prices for traditional ink-press printing and POD using a softcover (perfect bound), 144 page, 5.5 x 8.5, book with black text and a four-color cover:

—Press (ink on paper): $1.75 each, but you have to print 3,000 to 5,000 to get a price this low. So, your print bill will be at least $5,250.

—POD (single copies): May run $4 to $7 each and are often bundled with other services. But you can buy your books, as many as you like and as you need them, triple your investment, buy more books and pocket the profit.

Print-On-Demand started out as a good option when a book had run its course, the inventory was exhausted, and orders were still dribbling in a few at a time. But it soon became apparent to publishers that it made more sense to have their books produced as needed right from the start, rather than the always risky investment in inventory, warehousing, insurance, and maintenance, etc.

4. The quality of POD printing is actually better. There are no light and dark pages as in ink-on-paper printing. The density is maintained electronically, unlike offset printing where a variation of 5% to 10% is a regular occurrence.

5. POD books never go out of print and can be updated very easily and affordably. This is a godsend for academics and researchers in any field.

6. POD books can be printed in most countries, so there are no international shipping charges for the customers.

Customizing Your Book for Business

Because it is so easy and affordable to update and alter POD books, customization is also easy. You can renovate the cover of your books by adding your favorite sponsor's banner, or create a special cover for major holiday issues. If you've written a workbook, manual, text book or business book, you can tailor it to meet your target audience. If you make a premium sale to a company, it will cost just pennies to bind in a letter from the CEO or add the company logo to the cover. A few New York Times bestselling authors have even offered optional endings to their works of fiction. The options are virtually limitless. The book industry has matured to a new model. Today publishing is growing to be as dynamic and multifaceted as the knowledge and creativity it bares.

PART 3
A MARKETING PLAN

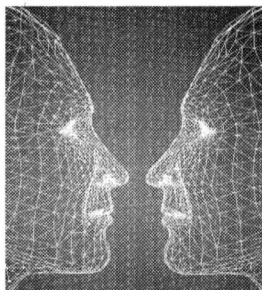

6

It's All About Networking

I mentioned earlier that when I started my career as an author, no one could have been more ignorant. My marketing plan consisted of traveling to as many cities as I could and doing as many book signings as I could set up. After 14 years of experience in the publishing world, this simple plan still remains the most effective. It is the one singular plan used by every successful publishing company in this industry: THE BOOK TOUR. Touring is the tried and true method for selling books, because ultimately, IT IS ALL ABOUT NETWORKING.

The book industry is basically a very grassroots industry. Word of mouth is responsible for 70% of all books sold. Most of the books that you have purchased in your lifetime were probably recommended to you by someone, either a friend, or over the radio, TV, or in school. A book tour allows authors to start the grassfires of marketing. When an author appears in a bookstore he or she meets the people who are interested in similar subject matter and genres. The bookstore personnel and the managers all listen to the author's presentation or reading, and if they like what they see they make it a point of keeping their shelves stocked with that author's books. Likewise, when the audience likes what they see and hear at a book signing, they want to talk to the author and invite them to their reading groups, church gatherings, classrooms, workshops, symposia, radio stations, TV shows, newspaper/magazine offices …and that is how it all begins. You just need to keep the process of networking alive and vital.

A good way to start spreading the news about your new book is to include a link below your email signature, so that every time you send email to someone you unobtrusively lead him or her to your online book-page (a must-have for authors). This opens the door for questions—"What is your book about?"—which can lead to more sales and networking. Some authors print an image of their books on business cards or send out postcards with their book cover on it.

There are thousands of ways to market a book without having to empty your savings account. Let your creativity and enthusiasm take the lead role.

The industry bible for successful book marketing is John Kremer's 1001 WAYS TO MARKET YOUR BOOK. www.bookmarket.com. This book is a must-read for every author.

> "Selling your books is essentially a matter of making friends, lots of friends"
>
> **—John Kremer**
> *Book Marketing Update*

@

7

The New Model for Promoting Your Book ...Simple is Best

> Visit to www.parapublish.com to check out Dan Pointer, pioneer and master of self-publishing

Using the new model for publishing, you are no longer printing a large quantity of books, enduring the shipping and handling costs, and then handing them over to fee-based distributors on a consignment basis. You no longer need to promote your book the traditional way: sending out expensive press packets, flyers and at least 500 review copies of your book to the elite media members of Don't-Call-Us-We'll-Call-You.

Today's authors build a website and use broadcast email to

invite reviewers and potential buyers to come to their sites to see, try or buy books or services. Promoting electronically saves you the expense of printing and postage fees and is significantly faster. You will often receive responses, sales or inquiries the same day.

Do Not Hire Spammers

Broadcast email, done properly, is not spam. Send your book announcements only to friends, customers, reviewers, opt-in lists, and members of the press. Don't be afraid to ask friends, or anyone you feel comfortable with, to send your broadcast email to everyone on their list. People love to help other people, but generally don't know how. Let them know what they can do to help you. Ask them to review your book on your website, or Amazon's website and all the retail book sites. Get the networking process started.

Keep your website simple, but include the necessary information to help your potential customer make a buying decision.

1. An image of the front book cover.
2. An annotation for the book.
3. Special features of the book or additional services or products.
4. An author photo.
5. Author bio.
6. Contact information.
7. Most Important: a link to buy the book.

> It is better to have a link on your site that allows customers to purchase the book elsewhere, otherwise you will be overwhelmed with processing credit cards, shipping, billing, inventory, damage returns, doing customer service, etc. Let us help you sell your books:
>
> www.1stworldpublish.com/bookstore

If you need help setting up your web site on this model, see www.1stworldpublishing.com/webservices or email info@1st-worldpublish.com.

When pitching your book to the media, email the entire ebook or egalley along with your promotional materials. Entice them and invite them to review your book or do an author interview. Emphasize your message or the storyline of your work. Each time you receive a review or a testimonial, post it to your website so others will see who is talking about you and your work.

Add the reviewer to your contact list and notify him or her directly when you are promoting your next book.

> *Publishers Weekly* and *USA Today* started reviewing their first egalleys in 1998.

Today many Reviewers prefer egalleys as they conveniently solve the solid-paper-waste disposal challenge.

Surf the Web: Find sites that relate to your own work. When you find a match, contact the owner and recommend an exchange of links. It's all about networking.

Participate in newsgroups: Get involved and meet people who share your interests and pursuits. Cut and paste your relevant content right from your book. For a list of newsgroups, see http://www.excite.com and http://www.deja.com.

For more ideas on promoting your books, read 1001 Ways to *Market Your Book* by John Kremer www.bookmarket.com and dozens of great books by Dan Poynter www.parapublishing.com

> **Book writing, publishing, selling and promoting has changed for the better. Now, authors, publishers and readers come out on top.**

1st WORLD
PUBLISHING
Publish it Now

www.1stworldpublishing.com

PART 4

A LITTLE KNOWLEDGE ABOUT THE PUBLISH-ING INDUSTRY

(A tutorial for 1st World Publishing)

8

Authors' Detailed Publishing Tutorial

There's a lot of information to absorb here. Don't be put off—we just want to make sure that you have a ready reference for all the details that can go into publishing. 1st World is here to guide you through the process every step of the way, to make sure that you use only those services you need, and that your results are satisfactory.

Steps in the Publishing Process:

1. Concept Validation

2. Coauthoring or Ghostwriting

3. Manuscript Evaluation

4. Manuscript Preparation

5. Title Selection

6. Manuscript Editing

7. Manuscript Layout

8. Manuscript Copyediting

9. Proof Production

10. Proof Editing

11. Cover Concept & Design

12. Cover Editing

13. Cover Production

14. Cover Copyediting

15. Match Print Production

16. Match Print Evaluation

17. Book Production & Shipping

18. Warehousing & Distribution

19. Marketing & Sales

1. Concept Validation

1stWorld Publishing's professional editors will discuss your book concept with you to determine its potential. This is an honest evaluation and is based entirely on what you hope to accomplish by writing and publishing your book. There is a difference between writing a book for posterity, as support for a personal/career goal or an organization's goals, or writing a book to be on the New York Times bestsellers list.

The big difference between having this discussion with 1stWorld Publishing and having the same conversation with a traditional publisher is that we are not going to be judging your concept on our ability to market and sell it. We know how difficult it is to market and sell a new book, especially one that is original. We will candidly share this hard-to-hear knowledge with you. The ultimate success of your book depends on your efforts to "get the word out." We make that very clear when you decide to use our services. But we don't leave it all up to you. We provide professionally lead seminars and workshops on every phase of book development, including promotion.

However, we also know that most of what is new and wonderful is missed when it's seen by the professionals who "know" what's selling, or know what they can sell. Here's a list of just a few books the world would never have seen had the authors listened to the pros: *The Hunt for Red October, Jonathan Livingston Seagull, Zen and the Art of Motorcycle Maintenance*, and *Chicken Soup for the Soul*. While our major objective is to help you realize your goal of seeing your book in print, we are also excited about the opportunity to discover and publish more of the world's "hidden gem" books-those which may have been turned down by the first few (or more) publishers the authors approached.

Here is a list of well-known self-published authors: www.bookmarket.com/selfpublish

2. Coauthoring or Ghostwriting

1stWorld Publishing employs professional writers who are ready to work with you on your manuscript. Ghostwriting works best if your book is autobiographical or related directly to your work and the lessons and experiences you wish to share. Coauthoring is also ideal for fiction writing when you have the story well in mind but do not believe you have the skill to write the book. Our writers can help you regardless of your situation.

3. Manuscript Evaluation

"How much will it cost me?" This is almost always the first question we are asked. The complete answer is not a simple one. This is why we have the Manuscript Evaluation step in the process. Every book is different; therefore, there is no way we can provide an accurate quote at the beginning of the process. The total cost will depend on a number of factors, including: the condition of your manuscript (how much editing it needs), any special treatments (graphics, page size, type of paper), the number of pages, and more. We cover all of this in the Manuscript Evaluation. When this is finished, you will have a very good idea what the total cost will be. We are determined to set your expectations straight, so that you will not be unpleasantly surprised as the process evolves.

4. Manuscript Preparation

1stWorld Publishing offers workshops and consultations in manuscript preparation to assist you in writing the first draft of your book. We have general writing workshops as well as those specifically geared to the type of book you are writing: historical, business, self-help, mystery, science-fiction, adventure, romance, children's, whatever your genre might be. An author published in the genre teaches each workshop.

5. Title Selection

Coming up with the right title for your book is an important step in the process. Your title will directly impact your book's market and shelf appeal. If you are comfortable handling this step yourself, we encourage you to take it on. If you would like our assistance, we have the creative staff available to ensure the title you choose is the right one. Choose a "working title" to begin with; the title can, and often does, evolve with the manuscript.

6. Manuscript Editing

Once your manuscript's first draft is completed, you will need a professional editor. 1stWorld Publishing will assist you in choosing the ideal editor for your project from our team of professional editors. This will ensure a strong, committed relationship that will ultimately lead to a flawless finished manuscript.

7. Manuscript Layout

Preparing the manuscript for publication can be a daunting task. The good news is that our process makes it easier than it's ever been. Our layout professionals ensure that your book will be produced with the same high standards and quality as with a traditional publisher. Your book will look as crisp and professional as any other publication on the shelves of bookstores across the country.

8. Manuscript Copyediting

This is one task you can't do yourself, although you will want to be involvedthe more eyes, the better the final product. Copyediting your own work is like representing yourself in court—t's just not a good idea. We have skilled professionals ready to help you with this difficult task. Be prepared for a number of iterations; it's just part of the process, and you'll benefit in the long run. Our standards are high. We won't let you down.

9. Proof Production

This step is handled by the printers. 1stWorld Publishing works with one of the finest digital printers in the business, so you can be sure your book will be of professional quality.

10. Proof Editing

Once we receive the proof, we will check for major errors. Then, you're nearly ready to print.

11. Cover Concept & Design

Cover design is critical. You may know exactly how you want your cover to look. You may have even done a prototype. However, you will want a professional graphic artist to design your cover so you can be sure to get professional results. Our marketing professionals know what a cover needs to say and how it needs to look to attract readers who will be interested in what you have written. The front cover needs to make the book jump off the shelf and into the reader's hands, while the back cover needs to encourage him or her to make the purchase. Again, we cannot overemphasize the importance of an attractive, effective cover. Let our experts help you.

12. Cover Editing

It is essential that the cover contains complete and accurate information needed to accomplish its purpose. Our skilled editors will make sure this happens.

13. Cover Production

Again, our professionals will accomplish this task for you. 1stWorld Publishing has an array of talented artists and designers available to ensure your cover is produced at a professional quality worthy of the effort you have put into your book.

14. Cover Copyediting

We will make sure your cover is exactly as designed before it goes into final production.

15. Match Print Production

This step is handled by the printer. See Step 9.

16. Book Production & Shipping

This step is handled by the printer (see Step 9). All you have to do is open the box when the final books are delivered to your door.

17. Warehousing & Distribution

1stWorld Publishing offers complete fulfillment and distribution services, for which we charge a very reasonable fee. Included in the price is the ISBN number, which is essential if you hope to sell your book through the retail channel, and the Library of Congress Number, which is needed before libraries will purchase your book. Additionally, we will see that your book gets listed in *Books in Print*.

19. Marketing & Sales

1stWorld Publishing provides Marketing and Sales Consultations by some of the top experts in the field, to equip you with solid ideas for marketing your book. However, we do not do the marketing and sales for you. If you like, we will set up a marketing campaign to fit your budget, but you must be integrally involved in the process or both your time and money will be wasted.

One of the little known facts about the publishing business is that, as a new author, you are expected to create interest in your book yourself. It is rare for a new author, even a previously published author, to be allocated the services of the publisher's sales and marketing department. Almost always their primary focus is on proven authors who have had, or are expected to have, a book on the bestseller list in the near future.

9

Read the Fine Print

Publisher Comparison Chart

Standard Service Offered	Self-Publish Vanity Press (Always watch for hidden costs)	Traditional Publishing	1st World Publishing
Will I get a FREE manu-script evaluation?	No	No	Yes (FOR A LIMITED TIME ONLY)
What Gets Published?	Soft Cover Edition (Pay extra for each edition if offered at all)	Soft Cover Edition	You Get 3 Editions Soft Cover — Hard Cover — eBook
How much roy-alty do I earn?	5 -10%	5%	50% Profit Sharing
Do I retain the copyright to my book?	Normally No	No	Yes

Do I get an Author /Book Marketing Web Page? (Author Biography with Photo and Book Promotion details)	No	No	Yes
Will my book be available through bookstores and online at Barnes & Noble, Amazon, etc?	Normally No	Yes	Yes
Will my publisher send out promotional press releases to over 300 newspapers and websites?	No	No	Yes (Monthly for actively selling titles)
Will I be registered and assigned an ISBN number?	Pay extra	Yes	Yes
Will I be registered with the Library of Congress?	Pay extra	Yes	Yes
Will I be able to purchase any number of copies of my book at a reasonable price?	No	No	Yes
Page Layout	Pay Extra if offered at all	Yes (no creative control)	Yes (You maintain creative control)
Cover Design	Pay Extra if offered at all	Yes (no creative control)	Yes (You maintain creative control)
Proof Reading	Pay Extra if offered at all	Yes	Yes (You maintain creative control)
Copyediting	Pay Extra if offered at all	Yes (no creative control)	Yes\Extra Charge We work with a full range of editors and each manuscript is individually evaluated and priced. (You maintain creative control and work directly with your editor.-the way it should be).
Content Editing	Pay Extra if offered at all	Yes (no creative control)	Yes\Extra Charge We work with a full range of editors and each manuscript is individually evaluated and priced. (You maintain creative control and work directly with your editor.-the way it should be).

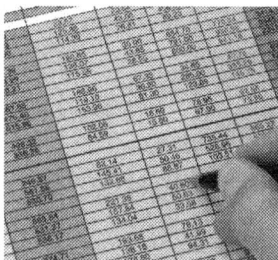

10

Publishing Industry Statistics

"Averages don't always reveal the most telling realities. You know Shaquille O'Neal and I have an average height of six feet."
                          —Robert Reich, U.S. Labor Secretary

(Robert Reich, 4ft. 10 inches / Shaquille O'Neal, 7ft. 1inch)

Book industry data may help you with your writing and marketing plans. Compliments of Dan Poynter: www.para-publishing.com/sites/para/resources/statistics.cfm

Number of Publishers

- ❖ 6 large publishers (in New York)
- ❖ 3-400 medium-sized publishers
- ❖ 86,000 small/self-publishers

❖ The six U.S. conglomerate publishers are

1. Random House, Inc.
2. Penguin Putnam Inc.
3. HarperCollins
4. Holtzbrinck Publishing Holdings
5. Time Warner
6. Simon & Schuster, Inc.

—*PMA Newsletter, September 2003*
http://www.PMA-online.org

❖ 8,000-11,000 new publishing companies are established each year.
❖ 2002: 10,000 new publishing companies were established. An increase of 15%.
—*Publishers weekly, June 2, 2003.*
http://www.PublishersWeekly.com

Who is Publishing how many Books?

❖ 78% of the titles published come from the small/self-publishers.

http://www.pma-online.org/benefits/industry_reports.cfm

❖ 2002: The five large New York publishers accounted for 45% of the market (made 45% of the sales.)
—*Publishers Weekly, June 16, 2003.*
http://www.PublishersWeekly.com

Book Sales

❖ United States: 2000: 80% of the book sales are controlled by five conglomerates: Bertlesman (Random House), Rupert Murdoch's News Corp, Time Warner, Disney and Viacom/CBS.
—*Andre Schiffrin, The Business of Books in the Washington Post. October 18, 2000.*

❖ 2002: Five large New York publishers had US sales of $4.102 billion and worldwide sales of $5.68 billion.

Random House: $2.1 billion worldwide
Penguin Group: $1.3 billion
HarperCollins: $1.1 billion
Simon & Schuster: $690 million (est)
AOL/Time Warner: $415 million
—*Publishers Weekly, June 16, 2003*
http://www.PublishersWeekly.com

❖ 2001: ~$25.4 billion **Trade books** (those in bookstores). ~$6.4 billion **Religious.** ~$1.3 billion **Professional.** ~$4.7 billion **Book Clubs.** ~$1.3 billion, and other categories.
—*Association of American Publishers*
http://www.publishers.org/industry/index.cfm

❖ 2002: Books sales totaled roughly $26.9 billion.
—*Association of American Publishers.*
http://www.publishers.org/industry/index.cfm

❖ 2002: A 5.5% increase over 2001. 2001 had a 0.6% increase over 2000.
College texts up 12.4% to $3.9 billion
Mass-Market paperbacks up 11.7% to $1.73 billion

Trade books up 8.8% to $6.93 billion
—*Publishers weekly, March 10, 2003.*
http://www.PublishersWeekly.com

❖ One-third of the books sold worldwide are sold in the US.
—*Overseas Book Service, December 8, 1998.*
http://www.overseasbookservice.com

❖ The top ten US cities by dollar volume of book sales and
number of bookstores are Los Angeles-Long Beach; New
York; Chicago; Boston; Washington, Philadelphia; San
Francisco; Seattle-Bellevue-Everett; San Jose; San Diego.
—*Christian Science Monitor, December 9, 1997.*
http://www.csmonitor.com

❖ A successful fiction book sells 5,000 copies.
—*Authors Guild.* http://www.authorsguild.org/

❖ A successful nonfiction book sells 7,500 copies.
—*Authors Guild.* http://www.authorsguild.org/

❖ **Australia**: Sales: A$1.26 billion (USD $820 million)
Sales of titles originating in Australia: A$747.7 million
(USD $486 million)
—*Australian Bureau of Statistics study of 228 publishers,
2000-2001.*

❖ **Canada**: Sales $2.4 billion. Foreign Rights. $313 million.
(Canadian Dollars)
About 50,000 titles are published each year.
—*Publishers Weekly* http://www.PublishersWeekly.com

* These figures are most likely understated.

eBooks

❖ eBook sales increased 1,442% in January 2003 over January 2002.
—*Publishers weekly, March 24, 2003.*
http://www.PublishersWeekly.com

❖ 70% of book fair visitors are ready to buy electronic books if they can run them on any computer. 67% are ready to read the, 62% would borrow them from a library.
—*Open E-Book Forum as reported in Booktech the Magazine, January/February 2003*

Bookstores

❖ 15,000 stores in the U.S. that carry books.
❖ 59% of the customers plan to purchase a specific book when entering a bookstore.
—*Book industry Study Group. Publishing for Profit by Tom Woll, page 170.* http://www.BISG.org

❖ 40% make impulse purchases.
—*Book industry Study Group. Publishing for Profit by Tom Woll, page 170.* http://www.BISG.org

❖ 2002: Of the $23.7 billion spent on books, only $10.7 billion is spent in bookstores. The non-traditional outlets sell more books.
—*Tami DePalma, Marketability.* twist@marketability.com

❖ Borders 2002: opened 41 super stores for a total of 404.
—*Publishers weekly, March 17, 2003.*
http://www.PublishersWeekly.com

Book Purchases by Store Type

❖ 24.6% Large chain stores
❖ 17.7% Book Clubs
❖ 15.2% Smaller chains and independent stores.
❖ 5.4% Internet such as Amazon.com
—*Book Industry Study Group.* http://www.BISG.org

❖ 2002: $450 million was spent on general-interest books at big-box stores such as Wal-Mart. That figure is up 7.4% from 2000. Costco and other price clubs are taking market share from the bookstores.
—*Ipsos Book Trends, reported in The Wall Street Journal, June 18, 2003*

❖ **Chain Stores - 2001 gross sales:**
Barnes & Noble: $3.8 billion
Borders Group: $3.5 billion
Books-A-Million: $443 million

❖ **Chain Stores - 2002 gross sales:**
Barnes & Noble: $3.7 billion
Borders Group: $3.4 billion
Books-A-Million: $443 million
—*Publishers weekly, April 7, 2003.*
http://www.PublishersWeekly.com

Online Bookstores

❖ Number of books sold online in 1999: 57 million.
—*The Standard, October 23, 2000.*
http://www.thestandard.com

❖ In 2000, online sales were 5-10% of total book sales. 40% were fiction.
—*The Standard, October 23, 2000.*
http://www.thestandard.com

❖ 2002: Online bookstores sold 10% of the books.
—*The Wall Street Journal, June 18, 2003*

❖ Amazon had 35.9 million visitors in May 2003. BarnesAndNoble.com had 7.9 million
—*ComScores Networks, Inc. The Wall Street Journal, June 18, 2003*

❖ Amazon.com sells 5% of all books for $3 billion. Amazon.com is ranked among the top 50 brands in the world.
—*Newsweek. April 9, 2001.* http://www.Newsweek.com

Consumer Spending in 1996

❖ $5.4 billion was spent on movies.
❖ 25.6 billion was spent on books.

Who is Buying Books

❖ Customers 55 and older account for more than one-third of all books bought.
—*2001 Consumer Research Study on Book Purchasing by the Book Industry Study Group,* http://www.bisg.org

❖ Only 32% of the U.S. population has ever been in a bookstore.
—*David Godine, Publisher.*

❖ 2001: Households purchasing at least one book 56.5%
—*Veronis, Suhler & Associates investment bankers*
http://www.veronissuhler.com

❖ The mean age of book buyers
1997: Age 15-39: 26.5% of the books bought
2001: Age 15-39: 20.8% of the books bought
1997: Age over 55: 33.7% of the books bought.
2001: Age over 55: 44.1% of the books bought
—*Ipsos NPD reported in Publishers Weekly, January 6, 2003*

Retail Book Buyers/Readers

❖ Women buy 68% of all books.
—*Lou Aronica, Senior V-P Avon Books. Publishers Weekly, March 22, 1999.* http://www.PublishersWeekly.com

❖ The median household income for book buyers is $41,600, compared to $35,300 for all adults.
—*Bookselling This Week, November 10, 1997.*
http://news.bookweb.org/

❖ Men are more likely to shop in chain stores than women. Women are more likely to shop in discount stores and super-markets than men.
—*Publishers Weekly, May 12, 1997, page 13.*
http://www.PublishersWeekly.com

❖ $1.7 billion is spent annually on textbooks. $78 billion is spent on alcohol, $37 billion on cigarettes and $6 billion on pet food.
http://bookbuzz.com/bisg1998study.htm

What genres/categories are people buying?

❖ 55% Popular fiction
❖ 10% Religious nonfiction
❖ 9% Cooking/Crafts
—*2001 Consumer Research Study on Book Purchasing by the Book Industry Study Group,* http://www.bisg.org

❖ 2002: Genres, quantity published.
New adult fiction: 17,000.
Juveniles: 10,000
—*R.R. Bowker in Publishers weekly, June 2, 2003.*
http://www.PublishersWeekly.com

Christian Books

❖ 2002 sales of books and products through all channels: just under $4.2 billion, up from $4 billion in 2000. $2.4 billion sold through Christian retail outlets; $1.1 billion through general retail; and $725 million through direct-to-consumer ministry channels.
❖ First 6 months of 2003: CBA member store sales were down 2%. Books increased 8%, Bibles increased 2% but music and gifts decreased 9%.
—*Christian Booksellers Association reported in Publishers Weekly, August 4, 2003* http://www.PublishersWeekly.com

Self-Help Books

❖ The self-help book category came into its own in 1936 with the publication of Dale Carnegie's book How to Win Friends and Influence People. Today self-help sales are $538-million and account for one in ten titles sold.
—*The Wall Street Journal, December 8, 1998.*
http://online.wsj.com/public/us

❖ 1,818 self-help titles were published in 1997, generating $538 million.
—*Simba Information as reported in USA Today.*
http://www.simbanet.com

❖ U.S. self-help books sell very well in Australia, moderately well in Japan and poorly in Britain. The majority of self-help books are purchased by women.
—*Bob Miller, Group Publisher of Hyperion as reported in USA Today.* http://www.USAtoday.com

Fiction

❖ 5,000 novels, 200 first novels and 100 scripts are purchased each year.
—*Ridley Pearson, Maui Writers Conference.*
http://www.ridleypearson.com

Screenplays

❖ A TV movie will be seen by 3-million people and will sell more books than a screen film.
—*Andy Cohen, Maui Writers Conference.*
GradeAProd@aol.com

Agents

❖ Eighty percent of the books published by major houses come through agents.
—*Michael Larsen, Literary Agent.* larsenpoma@aol.com

Advances

❖ 70% of the books published do not earn out their advance.
—*Jerrold Jenkins, 15 May 99.*
http://www.JenkinsGroup.com

❖ 70% of the books published do not make a profit.
—*Jerrold Jenkins, 15 May 99.*
http://www.JenkinsGroup.com

❖ Many advances are between $1,500 and $7,500.
—*Publishing for Profit by Tom Woll, page 109.*
TWoll@aol.com

❖ Gen. Norman Schwarzkopf received an advance of more than $5 million from Bertlesmann; Gen. Colin Powell got $6.5 million from Newhouse, Former O.J. pal Paula

Barbieri got $3.5 million from Time Warner. Simon &
Schuster, Random House, and Penguin Putnam wrote off at
least $100 million in unearned advances in 1996.
—*Bookselling This Week, October 6, 1997.*
http://news.bookweb.org/

❖ Large advances for books that flopped: Journey to Justice
by Johnnie Cochran, Ballantine paid a reported $3.5
million; Behind the Oval Office by Dick Morris, Random
House paid an estimated $2.5 million; Leading with my
Chin by Jay Leno, HarperCollins paid a reported $4
million.
—*The Wall Street Journal, May 29, 1997.*
http://online.wsj.com/public/us

Royalties

❖ The average royalty is 10.7% of net.
—*John Huenefeld. Publishing for Profit by Tom Woll, page
121.* TWoll@aol.com

Bestsellers

❖ Bestsellers accounted for 3% of the sales at Barnes &
Noble in 1997.
—*Business Week, June 29, 1998.*
http://www.BusinessWeek.com

❖ 64% of book buyers say a book's being on a bestseller list
is not important.
—*Publishers Weekly, May 12, 1997, page 13.*
http://www.PublishersWeekly.com

❖ Nearly all bestsellers come from five publishing conglomerates.
—*National Arts Journalism Program,* http://www.NAJP.org

❖ 2003. Harry Potter and the Order of the Phoenix by J.K. Rowling.
630 Barnes & Noble stores sold 286,000 copies in the first hour; 896,000 the first day.
1,200 Borders and Walden stores sold 750,000 copies in the first 23 hours; the highest first-day sales in its history.
In the UK, WHSmith sold 120,000 the first day. 31,500 postmen were needed to delver the book in England.
5-million copies were sold the first day, shattering all records.
—*The Wall Street Journal, June 2003.*

Returns

❖ Books are displayed in bookstores for one selling season of four months. Those books that do not sell are returned for a refund. Yes, books may be "gone today, here tomorrow." Returns are 21-23% for larger publishers according to the AAP.
—*Tom Woll in Publishing for Profit.*
http://www.publishers.org/industry/index.cfm

❖ Barnes & Noble had a return rate of 28% for all categories of books in 1996 and 19% in 1997.
—*Publishers Weekly Interactive. March 30, 1998.*
http://www.PublishersWeekly.com

❖ A return rate of 15% is considered very good.
—*Publishing for Profit by Tom Woll, page 76.*

❖ Sell-Through. Independent stores sell over 80% of the books they order. Superstores sell 70% of the books they order. Discounters such as Wal-Mart and Sam's Club sell about 60%.
—*The Wall Street Journal, May 29, 1997.*
http://online.wsj.com/public/us

❖ The industry return rate is 36.3% for hardcover and 25% for soft. B&N returns 19%.
—*Brill's Content, July/August 1998.*

❖ 2002: 37% of the books sent to stores were returned.
www.electronic-publishing.com

❖ Harper-Collins lost more than $250 million in a single year just on returns.
—*The New York Times, reported in Booktech the Magazine, March/April 2002*

❖ Up to 40% of all books manufactured never sell. Most publishers would rather suffer the costs of over-runs and returns than run short of a title.
—*Booktech the Magazine, March/April 2002*

Books in Print

❖ 2001: 1.5+ million titles in print (currently in the U.S.)
❖ Since 1776, 22 million titles have been published.
❖ About 120,000 titles are published each year.
—*Jerrold Jenkins, 15 May 99.*
http://www.JenkinsGroup.com

❖ 2002: Title output was up 5.8% overall. University press titles were up 10%.
—*Publishers weekly* http://www.PublishersWeekly.com

❖ 2002: Larger publishers decreased output 5% but titles published rose 6%.
—*R.R. Bowker in Publishers weekly, June 2, 2003.*
http://www.PublishersWeekly.com

❖ 2004: 2.8 million books in print.
—*R.R. Bowker as reported in The Wall Street Journal, April 24, 2004.*

Quantity of Publishers by Year

❖ 1947: 357 publishers
❖ 1973: 3,000 publishers
❖ 1980: 12,000 Publishers. The New York Times, February 23, 1981.
❖ 1994: 52,847 publishers. Books in Print.
❖ 2003: About 73,000 (plus those who publish through POD/DotCom publishers; they use the publisher's ISBN block.)

Book Printing

❖ 2003: Ingram's digital press prints (POD) 70,000 individual books/week. Their delivery channels cover more than 90% of the bookstores in the US. They fulfill nearly 1 million eBooks/day.
—*LightningSource* http://www.LightningSource.com

❖ Most initial print runs are 5,000 copies.
—*Publishing for Profit by Tom Woll. Page 113.*
TWoll@aol.com

❖ A larger publisher must sell 10,000 books to break even.
—*Brian DeFiore, Maui Writers Conference.*
http://www.defioreandco.com/

Covers, Book

❖ Everyone judges a book by its cover. On the average, a book store browser spends eight seconds looking at the front cover and 15 seconds looking at the back cover. Sales Reps show covers or jackets and give a sales pitch that averages 14 seconds. .
http://www.parapublishing.com/sites/para/resources/all-products.cfm

Libraries

❖ The library market was $3-billion in 1993. 68% of Baker & Taylor's sales are to libraries.
—*Jerrold Jenkins,* http://www.JenkinsGroup.com

❖ 90% of the 15,000 public libraries in the US order (some) of their books through Baker & Taylor and spend more than $444 million annually.
—*U.S. Department of Justice as reported in The Wall Street Journal, February 4, 1997.* http://www.ojp.usdoj.gov/bjs/

❖ Libraries lose 20% of their books each year. Some books get past the security devices and others are just not returned. http://www.ala.org

Book Fairs

❖ **Book Expo America 2001** had 2000 exhibitors http://www.BookExpoAmerica.com

❖ **The Frankfurt Book Fair** has 9,000 exhibitors. http://www.frankfurt-book-fair.com/en/portal.html

❖ 75% of the floor space at the 1999 BEA book fair in Los Angeles was occupied by small presses and self-publishers.
❖ Christian Booksellers Association Book Fair had 477 exhibitors in 2003
—*Christian Booksellers Association reported in Publishers Weekly, August 4, 2003* http://www.PublishersWeekly.com

Copyright Infringement.

❖ Global piracy losses to the U.S. book publishers estimated at $650.8 million in 2001.
—*International Intellectual Property Alliance.*
http://www.iipa.com/statistics.html

Writers and Authors

❖ 81% of the population feels they have a book inside them.
❖ 27% would write fiction.
❖ 28% would write on personal development
❖ 27% would write history, biography, etc.
❖ 20% would do a picture book, cookbook, etc.
❖ 6 million have written a manuscript.
❖ 6 million manuscripts are making the rounds.
—*Jerrold Jenkins. 15 May 99.*
http://www.JenkinsGroup.com

Literacy

❖ 1992: 20% of adults in the U.S. read at or below the fifth grade level.
—*National Adult Literacy Survey reported in Publishers Weekly, January 6, 2003.*

❖ "Half of the American people have never read a newspaper. Half have never voted for President. One hopes it is the same half."
—*Gore Vidal, author.*

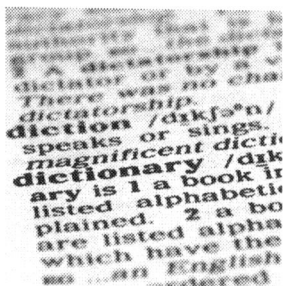

11

Glossary

Acid-Free Paper: Paper that is free from chemicals that destroy paper. It lasts longer, but costs more. It should be used for all books that are designed to be around for a few decades or longer.

Advance Copies: First books sent to those who ordered, requested or were promised a book, generally before the book goes into distribution. As a self-publishing author, it's always a good idea to try selling some advanced copies of your book.

Alignment: The position of text lines on a page. Left alignment means that the left margin of each line down the page is even, and that the right margin is ragged or uneven; right alignment means that the right margin is even down the page, and the left margin is ragged or uneven. Alignment can also refer to margins being justified, which refers to both left and right margins being even down the page, causing extra spacing between words when necessary. Center alignment means that the lines of text are centered down the middle of the page.

Artwork or Illustrations: Visual material, such as drawings, pictures, and photographs.

Back Matter: Printed material found in the back of the book after the main section of the book. This includes the appendix, the bibliography, the index, author's biography, etc.

Bar Code: The bar code is the ISBN number transferred into a worldwide compatible optical character recognition (OCR) form, the image made up of vertical lines that can be read by a scanner and identifies the title, author and publisher of the book. See ISBN.

Binding: The back and front covers and the spine that hold the pages of the book together.

Bluelines: The printer's photocopy or blue print mock-up of the book's pages. These are used by traditional publishers to detect errors and make corrections. On-demand publishing uses a Proof that is a copy of the actual book.

Body Copy: The main section of the book.

Body Text: The typed portion of a page, excluding the headline.

Boldface: Words or phrases in heavier and darker print used

for emphasis.

Book signing: An event usually held at bookstores or book fairs where the author reads, talks or discusses his/her book, providing an opportunity for potential buyers to meet the author and to have a copy of the book personally signed.

Cataloging in Publication (CIP): Card catalog information printed on the copyright page; a service provided by the Library of Congress for books extensively used in libraries.

Coated Paper: Chemically treated paper providing a glossy or matte finish used to enhance brightness.

Contract Publisher: An individual providing essentially the same services as a self-publishing services company.

Copyediting: The process of preparing the manuscript for the printer. At 1stWorld Publishing, the goal of the copy-editing process is to produce a final manuscript with very few grammatical errors (it's unreasonable to expect the book to be "error free") and complete accuracy regarding format-ting issues (page numbers, etc.).

Copyright: A legal notice that protects "original works of authorship" both published and unpublished. However, these works must be in a form accessible to others. You can't copyright ideas. The copyright is automatic and assumed from the moment the work is produced. However, it is easy for works to "slip into the public domain." All that needs to happen is for the author to "publish" without proper copy-right notification. Proper notification is a statement on the work that it has been copyrighted by the author and the date of the copyright, i.e. Copyright 2002, Fred Author.

Direct mail: Form of advertising by sending information (usually as a brochure or flyer) directly to potential buyers.

Distributor: A company that, for a fee, represents publishers by handling the warehousing and shipping of books to bookstores and libraries.

eBook: A book that is available in electronic format. Usually eBooks are available in Adobe PDF or eBook Reader format, or in Microsoft's LIT format.

Editing: The process where the manuscript is prepared for publication. At 1stWorld Publishing, the goal of our editing process is to produce an effectively written manuscript that communicates the author's message clearly.

Font: A particular typeface in a specific point size.

Foreword: Introductory remarks to the book written by someone other than the author.

Front Matter: Printed material found in the front of the book before the actual body copy starts. It includes title and copyright pages, dedication, foreword, preface, table of contents, etc.

Fulfillment House: A company that handles the entire ordering process for books, such as storing, packing, mailing, maintaining records, and other business related operations for the author or publisher.

Gutter: The white space formed by the inner margins of two facing pages.

Header: A caption or headline used to introduce chapters, sections or a new topic, usually in larger and bolder typeface than the body text.

ISBN Number: International Standard Book Number. This is the number that is used by booksellers to identify each book in stock. It's a worldwide identification system that is a required element in the book distribution industry.

Justify: Positioned lines of text so that the left and right margins are evenly set down the side of a page.

Layout: The overall design or mock-up of a page, including typeface, headlines, page number, and visuals showing how the page will look when printed; a guide for the printer.

Library of Congress Card Catalog Number LCCN: Established in 1901, a numbering system assigned by the Library of Congress, this number is used by libraries throughout the United States to identify each book in their stacks. Every book that is expected to sell to libraries must have a Library of Congress Catalog Number.

Manuscript: An author's written material ready for the final stages of production (editing, copyediting, etc.).

Marketing: The business of advertising, promoting and selling books to the public and to distributors.

Match Print: This is the final proof of a graphic before it is printed. At 1stWorld Publishing, Match Prints are used when producing the book cover. It is evaluated by the graphic artist in order to verify that the colors are identical with those in the original artwork.

Media Kit: Well-planned promotional materials, such as press releases, flyers, letters, and reviews used for announcing and circulating information about a forthcoming book.

Niche Market: An easily identifiable market that can be targeted for direct promotion, i.e. golfers, model plane hobbyists, collectors, etc.

Offset: The light image of transferred ink or an imprint that comes from an adjoining text page or illustration, or an inserted paper.

On-Demand Publishing: A relatively new technical process whereby the printing of the book is done entirely through a digital process that makes it possible to print any number of copies at a given time. With traditional printing , involving a typesetting process, it was necessary to produce relatively large quantities of a book to get the price down to where it could be sold through the retail channel. With on-demand printing, it is possible to produce short-runs of books at a cost that still enables sales through the retail channel and to libraries.

Overrun: To print a larger quantity of books than ordered. Printers estimate a 10 percent spoilage. If this does not occur, the additional books are charged to the customer but only up to 10 percent.

Perfect Bound: A binding method that uses plastic glue to bind the loose leaves to the book cover.

Press Release: A public relations announcement issued to the news media and other targeted publications for the purpose of letting the public know of company developments.

Printer: The company that prints and usually binds the book; in other words, produces the final product.

Proof: The first copy of the actual book, used to find errors and make necessary corrections.

Publicist: An individual or company who customizes promotional materials for a given book; may also assist in arranging public appearances and interviews.

Retail: The sale of books at full price directly to the public.

SAN: Stands for "Standard Account Number." A number assigned to libraries, schools and organizations that buy, sell or lend books.

Sans serif: Typeface that is straight with no serifs or small extensions on letters, generally used for headers.

Serif: The fine line that extends from the top and bottom of letters making them easier to read, used for the body text of a book.

Subsidy Press: See, Vanity Press

Target audience: An identified group of readers who would most likely be interested in a book's particular subject matter.

Title page: Odd-numbered page at the beginning of the book that gives the title, subtitle, author's name, publisher and place of publication.

Typeface: The style of typed letters used for the body text.

This text is in Times Roman.

Vanity Press: Companies that produce authors books at a price to the author, usually retaining all rights for a relatively long period of time (3 to 5 years), paying the author a royalty for any book sold during this time. During the licensing period the author must purchase from the Vanity Press any copies of the book needed for self-promotion. The actual royalty structure, or cost of books purchased by the author, differs with each Vanity Press, do policies regarding retail price, quantity discounts, etc. Vanity Presses are sometimes called Subsidy Presses.

Wholesaler: A company that handles the resale of books in large quantities and serves booksellers (distributors work on behalf of publishers).

About the Author

Rodney Charles is an innovative, self-motivated, entrepreneur and business leader who conceived the 1stWorld Publishing business while acting as President and Managing Editor of his own self-built book publishing company, Sunstar Publishing Ltd. (1992) His diverse experiences, ranging from media management, business-to-business aggregation and hands-on daily interaction with authors and publishers have resulted in the assembly of many of the resources required to implement 1st World. He has authored four books: *The Land of Love, Art & Genius; Lighter Than Air; The Secret Meaning of Names;* (editor) and the best-selling *Every Day a Miracle Happens.*

1st World Publishing
1100 North 4th Street
Gate Ridge Court Bldg.
Fairfield, IA 52556
tel/641/209-5000
Email: info@1stworldpublishing.com
Web: www.1stworldpublishing.com

* 9 7 8 1 5 9 5 4 0 8 4 5 7 *